The Conifer Division

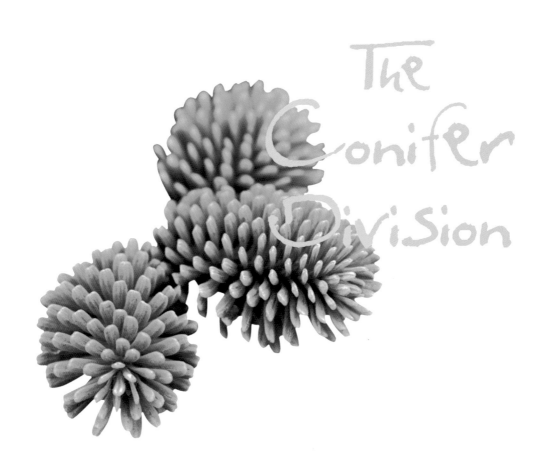

The Conifer Division

REBECCA STEFOFF

Marshall Cavendish
Benchmark
New York

Marshall Cavendish Benchmark
99 White Plains Road
Tarrytown, New York 10591
www.marshallcavendish.us

Editor: Karen Ang
Publisher: Michelle Bisson
Art Director: Anahid Hamparian
Series Design by: Patrice Sheridan

Library of Congress Cataloging-in-Publication Data

Stefoff, Rebecca, date
The conifer division / by Rebecca Stefoff.
p. cm. — (Family trees)
Includes bibliographical references and index.
Summary: "Explores the life cycles and other characteristics of plants, trees, and shrubs in the Conifer
division"—Provided by publisher.
ISBN 978-0-7614-3077-3
1. Conifers—Juvenile literature. 2. Biology—Classification—Juvenile literature. I. Title.
QK494.S68 2009
585—dc22
2008023373

Front cover: A conifer forest
Title page: Needles from a monkey puzzle tree
Back cover: Arborvitae

Photo research by Candlepants, Incorporated
Cover Photo: Martin Bond / Peter Arnold Inc
Alamy Images: Susan E. Degginger, 2, 59(left); fotoFlora, 12(left); PHOTOTAKE Inc., 21; PjrFoto /studio, 23;
Niall Benvie, 25; blickwinkel, 31, 50, 71; Edward Parker, 35; mediacolor's, 38; Photodisc, 39; K-Pix, 40; Arco
Images GmbH, 42; Organica, 44; Piotr & Irena Kolasa, 45; Kim Karpeles, 57; FLPA, 59(right); David R. Frazier
Photolibrary, Inc., 69; isifa Image Service s.r.o., 72; Chris Laurens, 78; Emmanuel Lattes, 79; Arch White, 81;
Imagebroker, 83. Corbis: Mark E. Gibson, 6; Hal Horwitz, 12(right); Richard Cummins, 32; Terry W. Eggers,
56; Ian Beames; Ecoscene, 64; David Muench, 74; Francis G. Mayer, 76. Shutterstock: 7, 19, 33, 51, 75, back
cover. AP Images: Julie Jacobson, 8. Photo Researchers Inc.: Frances Evelegh, 10; Francois Gohier, 18; Laurie
O'Keefe, 26; Biophoto Associates, 29, 55; Michael P. Gadomski, 58, 62(left); Biology Media, 61; Cristina
Pedrazzini, 62(right); Robert J. Erwin, 63; Stephen Collins, 65. Peter Arnold Inc.: John Cancalosi, 34; BIOS Bios
- Auteurs (droits gérés) Pascal André, 37; Reinhard, H., 41; Biosphoto / MG de Saint Venant, 47. Getty Images:
Keren Su, 46; Gary Cralle, 52; Louie Psihoyos, 54; Mark Moffett/Minden Pictures, 67. Minden Pictures:
Thomas Mangelsen, 82.

Printed in Malaysia
1 3 5 6 4 2

CONTENTS

The top of a redwood tree towers high above the children who marvel at the size of its broad base. The world's tallest trees are found among these conifers along North America's Pacific coast.

Classifying Life

When fog and rain drift inland from the Pacific Ocean to southern Oregon and northern California, they bring moisture to a low but rugged range of coastal mountains. On the green slopes of this coastal range grow towering trees called coast redwoods. One California redwood, a giant known as Hyperion, is the tallest tree in the world, measuring 379.1 feet (115.5 meters) in height.

East of the coast mountains rises the Sierra Nevada, a spine of mountains that runs through California and Mexico. In a few places in these mountains stand groves of giant sequoias. Sometimes called giant redwoods or mountain redwoods, sequoias are close relatives of the coast redwoods. Sequoias are not as tall as coast redwoods, but they are thicker and more massive. The biggest of all trees in terms of volume is a sequoia called General Sherman, located in California's Sequoia National Park. Researchers have estimated the total volume of this mighty tree's stem, or trunk, at 52,018 cubic feet (1,473 cubic meters).

The White Mountains are still further east, near California's border with Nevada, just north of Death Valley. They lie in the rain shadow of the Sierra Nevada, which means that the Sierras capture most of the rain from

In 2002 these forest researchers hiked the Methuselah Walk trail in Inyo National Forest, California, to gather cones and cuttings from a bristlecone pine that is more than 4,700 years old. The materials they collected may one day be used to clone the tree, the world's oldest known living thing.

the west, creating dry conditions on their east side. Too arid for redwoods or sequoias, the windswept, cold peaks of the White Mountains support hardy, slow-growing Great Basin bristlecone pines. One of these trees, called Methuselah after a long-lived biblical character, is the oldest known living thing in the world. It has been growing for more than 4,700 years.

The tallest tree, the most massive tree, and the oldest tree—all three of them belong to a group of plants called conifers, 600 or so species of plants that bear their seeds in cones. Some conifer species have formed vast northern forests that now support timber industries that provide wood and pulp. The conifer category also includes Christmas trees, miniature trees and shrubs used in ornamental gardening, and even a few plants that yield food items. To understand how these different kinds of conifers are related to each other, and how they fit into the natural world, it helps to know something about how scientists classify living things.

THE INVENTION OF TAXONOMY

Science gives us tools for making sense of the natural world. One of the most powerful tools is classification, which means organizing things in a pattern according to their differences and similarities. Since ancient times, scientists who study living things have been developing a classification system for living things. This system is called taxonomy. Scientists use taxonomy to group together organisms that share features, setting them apart from other organisms with different features.

Taxonomy is hierarchical, which means that it is arranged in levels. The highest levels are categories that include many kinds of organisms. These large categories are divided into smaller categories, which in turn are divided into still smaller ones. The most basic category is the species, a single kind of organism.

The idea behind taxonomy is simple, but the world of living things is complex and full of surprises. Taxonomy is not a fixed pattern. It keeps changing to reflect new knowledge or ideas. Over time, scientists have developed rules for adjusting the pattern even when they disagree on the details.

One of the first taxonomists was the ancient Greek philosopher Aristotle (384–322 BCE), who investigated many branches of science, including biology. Aristotle arranged living things on a sort of ladder, or scale. At the bottom were those he considered lowest, or least developed, such as worms. Above them were things he considered higher, or more developed, such as fish, then birds, then mammals.

John Ray, a pioneer of taxonomy, collected these plant samples in the seventeenth century. His plant collection contained specimens of about 18,600 species, including some conifers.

For centuries after Aristotle, taxonomy made little progress. People who studied nature tended to group organisms together by features that were easy to see, such as separating trees from grasses or birds from fish. However, they did not try to develop a system for classifying all life. Then, between 1682 and 1705, an English naturalist named John Ray published a plan of the living world that was designed to have a place for every species of plant and animal. Ray's system was hierarchical, with several levels of larger and smaller categories. It was the foundation of modern taxonomy.

Swedish naturalist Carolus Linnaeus (1707–1778) built on that foundation to create the taxonomic system used today. Linnaeus was chiefly interested in plants, but his system of classification included all living things. Its highest level of classification was the kingdom. To Linnaeus, everything belonged to either the plant kingdom or the animal kingdom. Each of these kingdoms was divided into a number of smaller categories called classes. Each class was divided into orders. Each order was divided into genera. Every genus (the singular form of genera) contained one or more species.

Linnaeus also developed another of Ray's ideas, a method for naming species. Before Linnaeus published his important work *System of Nature* in

1735, scientists had no recognized system for referring to plants and animals. Organisms were generally known by their common names, but many of them had different names in various countries. Two naturalists might call the same plant or animal by two different names—or use the same name for two different organisms.

To end the confusion, so that scholars everywhere could communicate clearly about plants and animals, Linnaeus started the practice of giving each plant or animal a two-part scientific name made up of its genus and species. These names were in Latin, the scientific language of Linnaeus's day. For example, the monkey puzzle tree's scientific name is *Araucaria araucana* (or *A. araucana* after the first time the full name is used). The genus *Araucaria* contains nineteen or so species of evergreen trees that are native to parts of South America, Australia, and some Pacific islands. The monkey puzzle tree, which originated in southern Chile and southwestern Argentina but is now used in many countries as an ornamental garden tree, is set apart from the other species in the genus *Araucaria* by the second part of its name, *araucana*.

Linnaeus named hundreds of species. Other scientists quickly adopted his highly flexible system to name many more. The Linnaean system appeared at a time when European naturalists were exploring the rest of the world and finding thousands of new plants and animals. This flood of discoveries was overwhelming at times, but Linnaean taxonomy helped scientists identify and organize their finds.

TAXONOMY TODAY

Biologists still use the system of scientific naming that Linnaeus developed. Anyone who discovers a new species can choose its scientific name, which is usually in Latin, or once in a while in Greek. Other aspects of taxonomy, though, have changed since Linnaeus's time.

Over the years, as biologists learned more about the similarities and differences among living things, they added new levels to taxonomy. Eventually, an organism's full classification could include the following taxonomic levels: kingdom, subkingdom, phylum (some biologists use division instead of phylum for plants and fungi), subphylum or subdivision, superclass, class, subclass, infraclass, order, superfamily, family, genus, species, and subspecies or variety.

Another change concerned the kinds of information that scientists use to classify organisms. The earliest naturalists used obvious physical features, such as the differences between fish and birds, to divide organisms into groups. By the time of Ray and Linnaeus, naturalists could study specimens in more detail. Aided by new tools such as the microscope, they explored the inner structures of plants and animals. For a long time after

Like all conifers, *Araucaria araucana*, the monkey puzzle tree (left), and *Juniperus virginiana*, sometimes called the eastern redcedar (right), bear their seeds in cones, although *J. virginiana*'s cones look like blue berries.

Linnaeus, classification was based mainly on details of anatomy, or physical structure, although scientists also looked at how an organism reproduced and how and where it lived.

Today, biologists can peer more deeply into an organism's inner workings than Aristotle or Linnaeus ever dreamed possible. They can look inside its individual cells and study the arrangement of DNA that makes up its genetic blueprint. Genetic information is key to modern classification because DNA is more than an organism's blueprint. DNA also reveals how closely the organism is related to other species and how long ago those species separated during the process of evolution.

In recent years, many biologists have pointed out that the Linnaean system is a patchwork of old and new ideas. It doesn't clearly reflect the latest knowledge about the evolutionary links among organisms both living and extinct. Some scientists now call for a new approach to taxonomy, one that is based entirely on evolutionary relationships. One of the most useful new approaches is called phylogenetics, the study of organisms' evolutionary histories. In this approach, scientists group together all organisms that are descended from the same ancestor. The result is branching, treelike diagrams called cladograms. These cladograms show the order in which groups of plants or animals split off from their shared ancestors.

None of the proposed new systems of classifying living things has been accepted by all scientists, but the move toward a phylogenetic approach is under way. Still, scientists continue to use the two main features of Linnaean taxonomy: the hierarchy of categories and the two-part species name. Experts may disagree about the proper term for a category, however, or about how to classify a particular plant or animal. Because scientists create and use classifications for many different purposes, there is no single "right" way to classify organisms.

Even at the highest level of classification, scientists take different approaches to taxonomy. A few of them still divide all life into two kingdoms, plants and animals. At the other extreme are scientists who divide life into thirteen or more kingdoms, possibly grouping the kingdoms into

Classifying a Christmas Tree

People have used many kinds of conifers as Christmas trees, but one of the most popular trees for that particular use is the balsam fir, *Abies balsamea*. Native to North America, the balsam fir is common across eastern and central Canada. It is the official tree of the Canadian province of New Brunswick. The tree also grows in the northern part of the United States, east of the Mississippi River.

Each winter, growers harvest hundreds of thousands of fragrant balsam firs and ship them to marketplaces, where they meet their destiny in the seasonal ritual of tree-shopping. Here is how a plant taxonomist classifies this Christmas tree:

Kingdom	Plants
Division/Phylum	Coniferophyta (woody, cone-bearing seed plants)
Class	Pinopsida (four orders of conifers; three extinct, one living)
Order	Pinales (all living conifers; seven families)
Family	Pinaceae (pine family; eleven genera)
Genus	*Abies* (firs; about 50 species)
Species	*balsamea* (balsam fir; also called blister, eastern, and balm-of-Gilead fir or Canada balsam)

larger categories called domains or superkingdoms. Most scientists, though, use classification systems with five to seven kingdoms: plants, animals, fungi, and several kingdoms of microscopic organisms such as bacteria, amoebas, and algae.

The classification of living things is always changing, as scientists learn more about the connections among organisms. In the case of conifers, for example, not all experts agree on how best to group the known species and genera into families and orders, or on exactly how conifers are related to their closest relatives in the plant kingdom. But although the details of conifer classification may change, one thing is certain: preserving the world's conifers for the future, while making use of the resources they offer today, is a conservation challenge.

PLANT KINGDOM

Scientists arrange living things into patterns to highlight the
This is one of several classifications

KINGDOMS

Animals

Plants

Fungi
(Fungi,
Lichens)

DIVISIONS

**Bryophytes
(Mosses)**

Polytrichum moss

**Sphenophytes
(Horsetails)**

Field horsetail

**Pterophytes
(Ferns)**

Brackenfern

**Psilophytes
(Whisk Ferns)**

**Lycopodophytes
(Club Mosses)**

FAMILY TREE

connections and differences among the many forms of life.
scientists have developed for the plant kingdom.

Monera
(Bacteria)

Protoctista
(Algae, Slimemolds, Protozoa)

Cycadophytes
(Cycads)

Sago palm

Coniferophytes
(Conifers)

Black spruce

Gnetophytes
(Gnetums, Ephedras,
Welwitschias)

Green Mormon tea

Ginkgophytes
(Ginkgos)

Ginkgo

Magnoliophytes
(Angiosperms or
Flowering Plants)

Lily of the valley

Paleobotanists—scientists who study the remains of ancient plant life—identified this fossil as cones of *Araucaria mirabilis*, a conifer that flourished in many parts of the world between 135 and 180 million years ago. It was closely related to living araucaria trees.

A World of Plants

In 2003, some students at the University of Illinois in Chicago took a field trip with a science professor to a limestone mine southwest of the city. There they found a cave that proved to be full of fossils. Four years later, after excavation and study, the professor and other researchers described some of the first finds from the cave. One striking discovery was conifer leaves—sometimes called needles—that date from around 310 million years ago.

If the researchers are correct in their dating, the leaves found in the Illinois cave are the oldest known conifer fossils in North America, and among the oldest in the world. From small but important pieces of evidence like the Illinois fossils, paleobotanists—scientists who study ancient plant life—are learning about the origins and development of conifers, which is just one chapter in the history of plant life on Earth.

THE ORIGIN OF PLANTS

The first living things on the planet appeared around 3.5 billion years ago, or perhaps even earlier. They were tiny, single-celled organisms in the oceans. Scientists call these cells prokaryotes, which means that they did not have an organized nucleus, or center. The early microorganisms were probably similar to prokaryotes that still exist today, such as the bacteria.

Bathed in the chemical-rich oceans, bombarded by sunlight and cosmic rays, the ancient prokaryotes exchanged fragments of their DNA and evolved into new varieties. By about 3.3 billion years ago, some of them contained a chemical called chlorophyll that gave them a green color and a new power. Organisms that contained chlorophyll did not have to absorb food from their environments. They could manufacture their own food—in the form of sugars—inside their cells from water, sunlight, and the gas carbon dioxide, which was plentiful in Earth's atmosphere. This process, known as photosynthesis, was a turning-point in the planet's history.

Photosynthetic microorganisms multiplied in the world's oceans, absorbing carbon dioxide from the air and giving off oxygen as a byproduct of photosynthesis. Over hundreds of millions of years, these photosynthe-sizing microorganisms changed the atmosphere of the planet. By lowering the level of carbon dioxide and raising the level of oxygen, they created the air that allowed oxygen-breathing life-forms to develop. Scientists believe that these photosynthesizing microorganisms of the ancient world were very similar to cyanobacteria, a type of photosynthesizing prokaryote that still exists today.

While photosynthesis was transforming the world, life reached another milestone with the appearance of complex cells, or eukaryotes. Unlike prokaryotes, eukaryotes are cells in which DNA and other substances are enclosed in a central structure called a nucleus. Like the prokaryotes, the first eukaryotes were microscopic, single-celled organisms. Between 1 billion and 800 million years ago, though, more complex organisms started to appear as eukaryotic cells joined together to form fronds or ribbons. Some of these organisms were green algae, the ancestors of all plants. For this reason, some taxonomists include the 7,000 species of green algae that exist today in the plant kingdom.

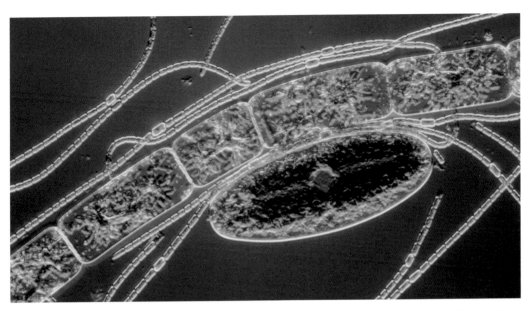

Cyanobacteria (thin, hairlike strands) are blue-green algae that scientist think resemble the first organisms that turned sunlight into food and oxygen through photosynthesis. These cyanobacteria share their aquatic habitat with two types of green algae: netrium (oval) and zygnema (string of square cells).

Plants were the first living things to move from water to land. To do so, they had to adapt to new conditions. Water performed many important functions for plants. It supported them; it protected them from becoming dried out or burned by the Sun; and it carried substances such as nutrients and gametes—the plants' reproductive cells—from one part of the plant to another. To survive on land, plants would need new kinds of cells and tissues to perform those functions.

Around 470 million years ago the necessary features began to appear in some green algae. One development was the cuticle, a waxy coating that helped protect exposed plants from drying out and from solar radiation. Gametes acquired protective coatings, too. Groups of specialized cells appeared, and eventually they formed structures through which water and nutrients could travel. Some paleobotanists think that these adaptations

Time Travelers in Amber

Some plants produce a liquid called resin, made of a combination of sugars, acids, alcohols, and other organic chemicals. Scientists do not know for certain what purpose resin serves, but it may serve to seal wounds or breaks in the plant's stem, or provide chemical defense against fungi, bacteria, and insect pests. Resin is so thick and sticky that it traps and holds seeds, small leaves, insects, or spiders that touch it. After the resin covers the insect or plant part, the sugars in the resin draw the moisture out of the object's tissues, preserving the dehydrated plant or animal inside a blob of resin. If the resin itself is preserved—perhaps by being buried in sand after the tree falls—it may turn into a fossil. Resin that has been fossilized is called amber.

Fossilization takes a long time. Most of the amber found today comes from trees that lived between 30 and 90 million years ago. And although conifers are not the only plants that make resin, much amber does come from ancient conifers, including araucarias, pines, and other trees that were related to the resin-producing conifers of the modern world.

Amber has long been prized as a gem. To paleontologists, however, amber's greatest value lies in what it may tell us about the plants and animals of the ancient world. Many chunks of amber contain flowers, leaves, seeds, pollen, mosquitoes, bees, beetles, and ants from millions of years ago. Scientists are interested in

Sticky tree resin trapped these flies between 40 and 50 million years ago. Now they are preserved forever in the fossilized resin, or amber.

organisms that have been preserved in amber because these remnants are more complete than stone fossils. Some insects taken from amber, for example, still have traces of body fluids, stomach contents, and parasites. In 1993, scientists obtained DNA from a leaf found in amber. The leaf, which belonged to a plant called *Hymenaea protera*, was 35 to 40 million years old. It is one of many organisms from the past that scientists have been able to study because of the remarkable preserving properties of resin.

took place in aquatic habitats that were dry for part of the time, such as along shorelines or in tide pools. Once green algae had adapted to life with periodic spells of dry conditions, they could move onto the empty continents and become fully terrestrial, or land-dwelling.

ANCIENT FORESTS

The oldest known fossils of land plants date from about 430 million years ago, although plants may have become terrestrial before that time. In their new environment, these algae-like plants evolved quickly into new forms. The earliest to appear were the bryophytes, a group of plants that includes mosses, liverworts, and hornworts.

Bryophytes lacked an internal system for carrying water and nutrients, so they thrived only in damp places, and they remained small in size. (This is true of the mosses, liverworts, and hornworts that exist today.) The bryophytes did, however, have one important adaptation to terrestrial life. Their reproductive cells took the form of spores, tiny particles that could be carried on the wind and could survive in dry, exposed conditions for some time. The spore was a reproductive leap forward for plants.

By about 408 million years ago vascular plants had evolved. These plants had internal structures made up of hollow cells that formed specialized tissues: xylem to carry water and minerals from the roots up through the stems and leaves, and phloem to carry the food produced by photosynthesis from the leaves to the rest of the plant.

The first vascular plants were the pteridophytes, a group that includes ferns, clubmosses, and horsetails. Other types of vascular plants evolved in the ancient world but, unlike the pteridophytes, they became extinct, with no descendants in the modern world.

Among the early pteridophytes were the lycophytes, a subgroup that contains the clubmosses, spikemosses, quillworts, and scaletrees. During a time that scientists call the Carboniferous period—between about 354 and

A bed of mosses includes sphagnums (red and yellow-green) and polytrichium (feathery bright green). Modern mosses are descended from the first land plants, the ancient bryophytes.

290 million years ago—lycophytes formed the world's first forests, enormous stretches of land covered with plants that grew to heights of 33 feet (10 m). Some plants were two or even three times that tall. As these forests spread across the land, more photosynthesis took place, and the rate at which oxygen replaced carbon dioxide in the atmosphere increased. The decrease in carbon dioxide, which is a greenhouse gas, gradually lowered temperatures around the world.

Vascular plants also began moving water through the environment in cycles. Gases, including water vapor, flow out of a vascular plant through tiny pores in the leaves. This outflow, called transpiration, creates a vacuum in the plant's vessels, and that vacuum sucks water upward from the roots, bringing fresh nutrients from the soil. Because vascular plants draw water out of the soil and release it into the air, a region's climate depends to a large extent on the number and kind of plants that grow there. By reducing the amount of water in the soil, the spreading Carboniferous forests slowly turned swampland into drier woodland.

Over millions of years, as the large plants of this period died, they formed deep deposits of vegetable matter. The passage of time and the pressure of new deposits bearing down from above hardened this dead vegetable matter into the mineral known as coal. Much of the coal that fueled the Industrial Revolution in the modern world came from the vast Carboniferous forests.

Like the bryophytes, the pteridophytes reproduced by means of spores. The next major development in plant evolution, however, replaced spores

The world's first forest had no trees. Instead, horsetails and other ancient plants towered above the landscape 300 million years ago. Insects—including *Meganeura*, a dragonfly with a wingspan of 2.5 feet (76 centimeters)—lived in the ancient forest.

with seeds. A seed consists of three parts: a fertilized reproductive cell, surrounded by nutrients to support the cell when it starts to grow, encased in a protective shell or coating. The first plants to produce seeds instead of spores appeared between 360 and 350 million years ago. By that time, plants no longer had the world's land masses to themselves. Arachnids, insects, and amphibians had already colonized terrestrial habitats, and other types of animal life would follow. Plants were part of an expanding ecosystem of living things.

THE RISE OF THE CONIFERS

Several kinds of seed plants existed throughout the Carboniferous period, but they were outnumbered by the lycophytes and other spore-bearing plants. After about 290 million years ago, however, the seed plants became more numerous—in both the number of species and the number of individual plants. By 260 million years ago, more than 60 percent of the plants in the world were seed plants. The spore-bearing plants that had dominated the Carboniferous forests were losing ground.

What caused the seed plants to overtake the spore bearers? Scientists are not sure, but many think that the explanation lies in climate change. By the end of the Carboniferous period, movements of the continental plates had created several large supercontinents and many mountain ranges. The result was a world in which more of the land was drier, hotter, and colder than it had been before. Seasonal changes, such as differences in temperature and rainfall, had also grown more extreme.

Seeds can survive prolonged periods of dryness, heat, or cold better than spores can, which gives seed-bearing plants some reproductive advantages over spore-bearing ones. As the Carboniferous period drew to a close, seed plants spread into dry, hot, or cold environments in which mosses, ferns, and other early plants could not survive.

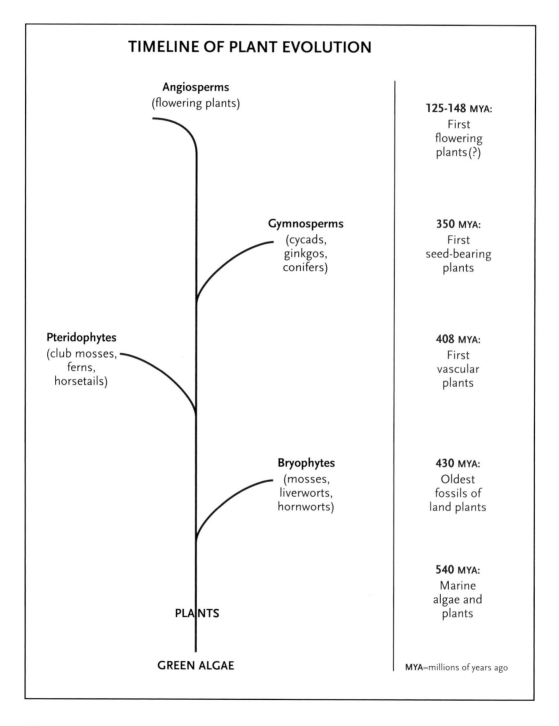

TIMELINE OF PLANT EVOLUTION

Angiosperms
(flowering plants)

125-148 MYA:
First flowering plants(?)

Gymnosperms
(cycads, ginkgos, conifers)

350 MYA:
First seed-bearing plants

Pteridophytes
(club mosses, ferns, horsetails)

408 MYA:
First vascular plants

Bryophytes
(mosses, liverworts, hornworts)

430 MYA:
Oldest fossils of land plants

540 MYA:
Marine algae and plants

PLANTS

GREEN ALGAE

MYA=millions of years ago

Between 315 and 300 million years ago several new types of seed plants appeared. Some of them eventually became extinct, leaving no descendants. Three kinds of seed plants that flourished after the Carboniferous period, however, are still represented in the modern world. They are the cycads, the ginkgos, and the conifers.

The oldest known fossils of cycads and ginkgos date from around 280 million years ago, although some paleobotanists think that these plants probably appeared millions of years before that time. Cycads today are found only in tropical regions, and ginkgos are native to China, but 240 million years ago forests of ginkgos and cycads thrived in many parts of the world. Fossils of these trees have even been found in northern areas such as Siberia and Greenland.

From fossils such as these ginkgo leaves, scientists have learned that ginkgo trees, which once grew in many parts of the world, were among the earliest known seed plants. Only one species survives today.

According to the fossil record, conifers existed by 310 million years ago. Scientists do not yet know for certain whether the conifers, ginkgos, and cycads all evolved from the same ancestral plants, now extinct. Some DNA studies suggest that conifers and ginkgos are more closely related to each other than to cycads. Whatever their origins, the early conifers shared important features with the conifers that exist today. They had simple root systems consisting of a single long root, called the taproot, that grew straight down, with smaller roots branching off it to the sides. They had woody stems and small, simple leaves, often resembling needles or flattened strips of scales. They bore their seeds in clusters that were usually cone-shaped. These seed cones are the source of the name *conifer*, which comes from the Latin words for "cone bearer."

Conifers were the dominant forest trees across the ancient world during the Triassic and Jurassic periods, from about 248 to 144 million years ago. Although many of these ancient conifer varieties disappeared without leaving descendants in the modern world, paleobotanists have traced the origins of all modern conifer families to the Triassic and Jurassic periods. The oldest of these surviving conifer families is the podocarps or yellow-woods. Representatives of this family appear in the fossil record about 248 million years ago. The youngest family, the plum-yews, emerged 160 million years ago.

FLOWERING PLANTS

Together the conifers, cycads, and ginkgos are sometimes called gymnosperms, from the Greek words meaning "naked seeds." The name contrasts these plants with the last major plant group to evolve, the angiosperms or "contained seeds." The seeds of angiosperms develop inside chambers called carpels. A carpel is a flower's female reproductive part, and as the seed ripens within it, it becomes a fruit.

Angiosperms—a group that includes grasses, shrubs, vines, most kinds of trees, and many other varieties of plants—are the only plants that produce flowers and fruit. Gymnosperms bear seeds without flowers or fruit. (Scientists traditionally grouped another division of woody plants, the gnetophytes, with the gymnosperms, but recent DNA research suggests that these plants are more closely related to angiosperms than to gymnosperms.)

Paleobotanists are still investigating the origins of flowering plants, but most agree that the first angiosperms appeared sometime between 148 and 125 million years ago. In evolutionary terms, they were a smashing success. Even though flowering plants are less than half as old as conifers, they overtook the conifers to become the dominant form of plant life in the majority of the

Autumn paints a landscape of mixed conifers and flowering plants. While conifers remain green, the leaves of most flowering plants turn red, yellow, or brown in the fall.

world's habitats. But although the conifers no longer rule the plant kingdom, they are by far the most numerous of the surviving gymnosperms, as well as the most economically important.

The pinyon pine is adapted to life in the stark canyons and mountains of the American Southwest and northern Mexico. Its nutritious seeds provide food for birds, animals, and people.

The Cone-Bearers

Botanists do not know for sure how many species of plants exist today. Their estimates range from 265,000 to 400,000. Whatever the total number of plant species may be, the overwhelming majority of them—more than 90 percent of all plant species—are angiosperms. The surviving pterido-phytes, in comparison, number about 10,000. Gymnosperm numbers are even less impressive, with 700 or so total species.

A single species of ginkgo, a Chinese tree called *Ginkgo biloba*, exists today. People in many parts of the world have used it as an ornamental tree. About a hundred species of cycads survive. These thick-stemmed plants are found in tropical or subtropical regions. The rest of the gym-nosperms are conifers.

Most botanists agree that all conifers belong to a single division or phy-lum, known as Coniferophyta or Pinophyta. In traditional taxonomy, the conifer division contains a single class called Pinopsida. That class includes several orders of extinct conifers and one order of existing ones, the Pinales. All living families of conifers belong to the order Pinales.

Advances in DNA studies, however, have thrown traditional plant tax-onomy into turmoil. Many botanists today regard the ranks of order and class as indefinite. Some of them think that several of the families should

In Arizona's Petrified Forest National Park, as well as other places around the world, visitors can see huge stone cylinders that are the fossilized, or petrified, trunks of ancient trees. These conifers date from the late Triassic period, about 215 million years ago.

be grouped into a new order. Meanwhile, most researchers focus their attention on the study of species, genera, and families. Although some botanists recognize six or eight families of conifers, a widely used system of classification divides the conifers into seven families.

THE FAMILY PODOCARPACEAE: PODOCARPS

The podocarps are a large family of 18 genera and more than 170 species of trees and shrubs. Some members of this family are called yellowwoods; that term, however, is also used for other, non-coniferous trees with yellowish wood.

Nearly all podocarp species are native to the southern hemisphere. Several kinds of podocarps grow in Africa south of the Sahara Desert, other types are native to Central and South America, and a few species occur in China and as far north as Japan. The great majority of species, however, are found on islands in the eastern and southern Pacific Ocean, including New Zealand, Tasmania, New Caledonia, Borneo, New Guinea, Indonesia, and the Philippines.

The totara is the largest tree in the podocarp family, and this New Zealand tree, called Pouakani, is the largest known totara. It stands 141 feet (42.7 m) tall.

Most podocarps are trees that favor wet environments in tropical or subtropical climates. The largest and best-known species in the family is the totara of New Zealand, *Podocarpus totara*. This slow-growing, thick-trunked tree can reach heights of more than 132 feet (42 m). The podocarp family also contains a few much smaller conifers. *Lepidothamnus laxifolius*, another New Zealand species, grows so close to the ground that it is called a creeper. It rarely reaches heights greater than 3 inches (8 centimeters).

The island of New Guinea is home to a podocarp called *Parasitaxus ustus*. This shrub or small tree attaches its roots to the roots of another tree, often a larger podocarp. *P. ustus* draws nitrogen and sugars from the host plant or from beneficial fungi that live among the host's roots and normally supply the host with nutrients. Because *P. ustus* does nothing to benefit its host and may actually harm the host, it is considered a parasite. This small, rare podocarp is the only known parasitic conifer.

THE FAMILY ARAUCARIACEAE: ARAUCARIAS

The araucaria family consists of about 40 species in three genera. Around 100 million years ago, araucarias grew in almost every part of the world. Arizona's Petrified Forest, a mass of fossilized araucaria trunks, is one remnant of that age. Today araucarias, like podocarps, are almost entirely limited to the southern hemisphere, except for those that humans have planted in other parts of the world.

Araucaria araucana, the monkey puzzle tree, is one of several species that grow in the mountains of southern South America. A few other species occur on the Malay Peninsula of Southeast Asia and in the Philippines. The greatest concentration of araucarias, however, is found in New Caledonia, New Zealand, and Australia. Large araucarias such as the New Zealand kauri, *Agathis australis*, which can be 99 to 165 feet (30 to 50 m) high and 3.5 to 13 feet (approximately 1 to 4 m) in diameter, are harvested for timber.

Araucaria heterophylla, the Norfolk Island pine, is now widely used as a houseplant (when it is young and small), an ornamental tree, a wind-break (especially in coastal areas, because this tree tolerates high levels of both salt and wind), and even a Christmas tree.

THE FAMILY CUPRESSACEAE: CYPRESSES

The cypress family, with 30 genera and 142 species, is found almost worldwide. The geographic range of this family, in fact, is greater than for any other family of conifers. Species of Cupressaceae grow in the Arctic, in the Sahara Desert, and high in the Himalayas of Asia. Although many species have small, limited ranges and are rare or even endangered, other trees and shrubs in this family are widespread and common.

During the nineteenth century the popular ornamental *Araucaria araucana* became known as the monkey puzzle because people said that even monkeys, those nimble climbers, would be puzzled to find a way through its spiky branches.

The Cupressaceae are a highly diverse family, and its members are known by a wide variety of common names. *Cupressus* and several other genera are made up of cypress trees. The genus *Taxodium,* for example, contains the bald cypresses, water-tolerant trees that grow in swamps in southern North America and develop knobby aboveground roots called

Bald cypresses can grow in dry soil, but their seeds cannot mature without a lot of moisture. As a result, bald cypresses are often seen on riverbanks or in swamps, where they thrive in year-round water.

knees. Other members of the family Cupressaceae are known as incense-cedars and redcedars, although they are not true cedar trees (which belong to a different conifer family). Trees and shrubs in the genus *Juniperus* are called junipers. They produce small, round, fleshy cones that are edible in some species. These edible cones, usually called juniper berries, are used for flavor in cooking and also in distilling the alcoholic drink gin.

Many members of the family Cupressaceae possess a feature that has given them great cultural and economic value. Their heartwood—the wood in the center of their stems or trunks—is not only fragrant but also resists the attacks of fungi and termites. People have turned to these species of Cupressaceae when they need wood that can survive exposure to soil and weather, for uses such as fenceposts, coffins, and "cedar" roof shingles and wall siding. *Thuja plicata,* the Western or giant redcedar, held a place of great importance in the traditional cultures of Native Americans throughout the Pacific Northwest. They made dugout canoes from the red-cedar's stems, built their houses with planks and posts made from its wood, and created clothing and utensils from its flexible bark.

Several genera in the family Cupressaceae have just one species. *Cryptomeria,* for example, contains only the species *C. japonica,* known as the sugi in Japan, where it is the national tree. Each of the three red-woods—the coast redwood, the giant sequoia or redwood, and the dawn redwood—is the only species in its genus.

The dawn redwood, *Metasequoia glyptostroboides,* was once known only from fossils. Scientists believed that the species had become extinct millions of years ago,

Tree farmers cultivate *Cryptomeria japonica,* or sugi, throughout Japan and China. Sugi is sold as an ornamental tree, and its reddish, aromatic wood is also prized for construction and furniture making.

The dawn redwood is one of the few conifers that is not an evergreen. In the fall, its green leaves turn brown and drop off the tree.

until a few scattered populations of living trees were discovered in China in the 1940s. Since that time the dawn redwood, which grows well in most temperate habitats, has become a popular ornamental tree. It is one of the very few deciduous conifers, which means that it sheds its leaves seasonally and all at once (the others are the bald cypresses and the larches). In addition to dawn redwoods, the junipers, cypresses, and arborvitae are the leading garden and ornamental plants from the family Cupressaceae. Of all conifers, these are the most important to the horticulture, or garden, industry.

THE FAMILY SCIADOPITYACEAE: THE UMBRELLA PINE

The family Sciadopityaceae contains a single species, *Sciadopitys verticillata*, the Japanese umbrella pine. Fossil evidence reveals that this species has existed for about 230 million years. All of its close relatives became extinct long ago.

In the umbrella pine's native country of Japan the tree is known as the koya-maki, and this name is now coming into use in other countries as well. The tree reaches a height of 66 to 99 feet (20 to 30 m). Its thick, soft, reddish-brown bark and its wood have a spicy fragrance. Umbrella pines have two kinds of foliage. Small brown scale-like leaves grow on the tree's trunk and branches, while long green photosynthetic leaves stand out from the ends of short stalks called shoots. Scientists think that this photosynthetic foliage may consist of modified shoots rather than true leaves. The umbrella pine's attractive appearance and its status as a "living fossil" have made it a popular tree for gardens and botanical parks in parts of the world that have the high rainfall and mild temperatures this species requires.

The Japanese umbrella pine shares an unusual feature with cacti, asparagus, and some other plants. Instead of leaves it has narrow, flexible segments of stem tissue called cladodes. The cladodes look and act just like leaves, even performing photosynthesis.

41

THE FAMILY TAXACEAE: YEWS

Yew trees used to be regarded as a separate order from all other conifers. Today, however, most experts consider them a family in the same order as the rest of the conifers, based on DNA studies. There are seventeen species of yews in five genera.

Yews are shrubs or small trees with many branches and flat, narrow, short leaves. The cones of yew trees are almost like small fruits. They contain a single seed each, covered by a thick leathery or pulpy coating called an aril. Birds eat these arils, spreading the seeds inside through their droppings.

Yews are found in many parts of the northern hemisphere and grow well in a variety of conditions. Because of their hardiness and their dense foliage, yews have often been used to make hedges. Another important use for some yew species is as a source of anticancer drugs made from taxanes, chemicals contained in the bark of

Dense and hardy, yews make good hedges and garden mazes. Yews are one of the evergreen varieties used in topiary, the art of sculpturing trees and shrubs into shapes.

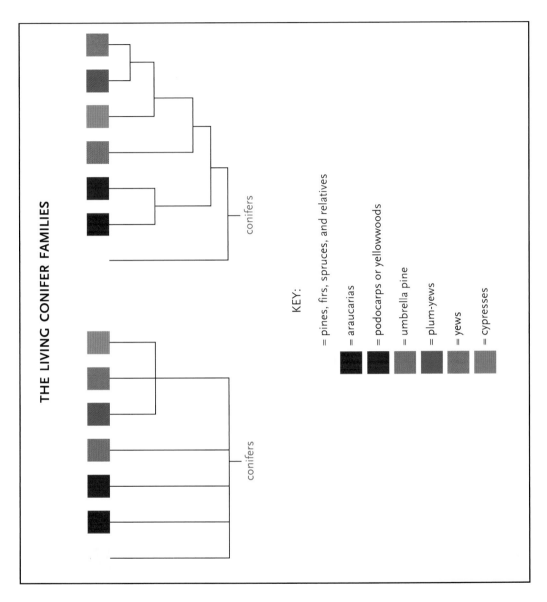

THE LIVING CONIFER FAMILIES

conifers

conifers

KEY:

= pines, firs, spruces, and relatives
= araucarias
= podocarps or yellowwoods
= umbrella pine
= plum-yews
= yews
= cypresses

Cladograms, or diagrams of evolutionary relationships, show two theories about how modern conifers are interrelated. The cladogram on the left shows five lines of descent from an ancestral conifer, with one line splitting into three families. On the right, pines and their close relatives descend directly from the ancestral conifer, while a second line of descent gives rise to the remaining six families. Scientists must carry out more research into plant genetics to know whether one of these theories is correct.

certain species, such as the Pacific yew. To meet manufacturers' needs and reduce the threat of overharvesting wild yew trees, some forest-products companies now grow yews on plantations.

THE FAMILY PINACEAE: PINES

The largest conifer family is the Pinaceae, with eleven genera and approximately 230 species. This family of conifers native to the northern hemisphere includes many of the world's most common conifers as well as some very rare ones. Botanists divide the Pinaceae into four subfamilies based on features of the plants' cones and seeds.

Tsuga canadensis, the eastern or Canadian hemlock, can become a forest giant if it receives enough sunlight. Shaded by larger trees, however, it may remain small and shrublike for years.

Although it sheds its leaves in the fall, the golden larch is not a true larch. It belongs to the *Pseudolarix* or "false-larch" genus. Like many other rare and unusual conifers, it is native to China.

The subfamily Abietoideae contains six genera. The *Abies* genus includes the firs, *Tsuga* contains the hemlocks, and *Cedrus* contains the cedars. The genus *Keteleeria* consists of three species found only in southern China and nearby countries. *Pseudolarix* is a genus with one species, the golden larch. *Nothotsuga* also has just one species, a rare Chinese conifer called the bristlecone hemlock.

The subfamily Laricoideae contains three genera: *Larix* for the larches, *Pseudotsuga* for the Douglas-firs, and *Cathaya* for the single species C. *argyrophylla*—another rare southern Chinese conifer. The subfamily Piceoideae consists of one genus, *Picea*, that includes the three dozen or so species of spruces.

The fourth and last subfamily in this family of conifers is the Pinoideae. It contains all of the pines in the world—between 110 and 115 species, mostly trees with a few shrubs. Botanists regard all pines as members of the same genus, *Pinus*, but they recognize two subgenera, one for typical pines and the other for white pines. Pine trees are native to almost every part of the northern hemisphere, but people have introduced them to many parts of the southern hemisphere as well. Various species are well adapted to cold, hot, or dry growing conditions. A few species, such as the bristlecone pine, grow at very high altitudes. Most species reach heights of 49.5 to 148.5 feet (15 to 45 m), but a few are taller. Small or low-growing species, such as the Siberian dwarf pine of northeastern Asia, may never grow taller than about 10 feet (3 m) and are often considerably shorter than that.

The Huangshan pine grows on the rugged granite peaks of eastern China's Huangshan Mountains. Chinese artists and poets have long celebrated the dramatic beauty of the region, which the United Nations has declared a World Heritage Site.

THE FAMILY CEPHALOTAXACEAE: PLUM-YEWS

The seventh and last family of conifers is the Cephalotaxaceae, or plum-yews. Botanists used to group the twelve to twenty species of plum-yews into the same family as the yews, but many experts now consider the plum-yews to be a separate family.

Plum-yews are small trees or shrubs found in the Asian nations of Korea, China, Japan, Burma or Myanmar, Laos, Vietnam, and India. People in some parts of this range have used plum-yews in traditional medicines. Like the yews, the plum-yews produce small berrylike cones that are covered by a fleshy aril. All known species are slow-growing plants that prefer shade. Their typical habitat is in the understory of moist forests, where they grow in the shade of taller trees.

Throughout their range plum-yews are uncommon or even rare. The cutting down of forests for the timber industry, or to clear land for farming, has put this conifer family—like many other conifers—at risk because of habitat loss.

Cephalotaxus harringtonia, the Japanese plum-yew, was the first plum-yew to be discovered and studied by Western scientists. Today it is found in botanical gardens around the world.

Climbing The World's Tallest Tree

A pair of hikers and amateur scientists discovered the world's tallest tree in the summer of 2006. Chris Atkins and Michael Taylor were exploring remote valleys in California's Redwood National Park when they came upon a grove of giant redwoods. One tree towered above the rest. The two men carried laser range finders, instruments that let them estimate the tree's height. At about 375 feet (113.6 m), it was a bit taller than the redwood known as the Stratosphere Giant, which had been regarded as the world's tallest tree ever since Atkins discovered it six years earlier. Atkins and Taylor named the new tree Helios after the Greek god of the sun.

Before Helios could be confirmed as the new tallest tree in the world, someone would have to climb it. Range finders provide good estimates, but records are set by accurate, hands-on measurements. A climber gets as close as possible to the top of the tree, then measures the distance that remains to the top. A weighted line dropped to the ground provides a second measurement. When the two measurements are added together, the result is the total height of the tree.

Atkins and Taylor knew that they would need more than measurements. They would also need witnesses who were not only reliable but able to keep a secret. Scientists and park officials do not like to reveal the exact locations of record-setting trees, for fear that the trees might be damaged by vandalism or too much attention (trampling the soil near the roots of redwoods and sequoias, for example, is bad for the trees). Atkins contacted his friend Stephen Sillett, a professor of botany who had studied the Stratosphere Giant. Sillett started getting ready to climb Helios, but before the climb took place Atkins and Taylor explored another valley and found a redwood even taller than Helios. They named it Hyperion, after the father of Helios in Greek mythology.

A few weeks later Atkins and Taylor led the way to Hyperion, accompanied by a group that included Sillett and another scientist, a tree climber, the chief ranger of Redwoods National Park, representatives of the Save-the-Redwoods League, and writer Richard Preston, who would later describe the adventure in his book *Wild Trees* (2007). After crawling through a pile of fallen redwood logs and pushing through tall ferns, they came to a trunk that was 15 feet (4.5 m) from side to side. They had reached Hyperion.

Sillett climbed up the tree until he estimated that he was about 20 feet (6 m) from the top. Up there the narrow stem was fragile, full of holes made by nesting birds. With an extendable metal rod Sillett measured the distance to the very top, and then he sent a measuring line down to the ground. Hyperion was 379.1 feet (115.5 m) from base to tip—the tallest tree in the world.

Norway spruce seedlings have sprung up next to a fallen tree in a German forest. The destruction of a mature tree by fire or windstorm lets sunlight reach the forest floor, creating opportunities for young trees to grow and repeat the conifer life cycle.

Lives of Conifers

Conifers share certain features that set them apart from other plants. Their anatomy, or physical structure, is distinctive, and so is their method of reproducing. Conifers also occupy unique ecological roles, creating food and habitat for other living things.

ANATOMY

Like other plants, conifers have three main structural parts: the roots, the stem, and the leaves.

Roots

A conifer's root system performs two functions: it absorbs water and nutrients from the soil, and it anchors and supports the plant. The root systems of conifers are generally fairly shallow, or close to the surface, but they may spread over a large area. An extreme case is the giant sequoia. The roots of these immense, heavy trees may extend over an acre but reach only 10 feet (3 m) into the ground.

Eastern arborvitae or whitecedar *(Thuja occidentalis)* manages to survive in harsh environments, thanks to a root system that can spread across cliffs where soil exists only in small pockets.

Sequoias and other large conifers with shallow root systems, such as coast redwoods and Douglas-firs, can be easily knocked over by powerful windstorms. Along the Pacific coast of North America, which is sometimes battered by strong winds from the ocean, conifer forests are typically full of downed trees. Mosses, ferns, and young conifers take root on the decaying logs of the fallen trees.

Stems

Conifer stems (often called trunks in the case of trees) and branches are woody. Like other woody plants, conifers are made up of several layers. The outermost layer is the outer bark, the plant's protective skin. Inside it is the inner bark, which contains phloem, the tissue that carries food from the plant's leaves to its branches, stems, and roots.

The innermost part of the tree, the heartwood, is dead, although it does not start to decay until the outer layers are broken in some way. Heartwood is made up of long fibers of the woody material cellulose, held

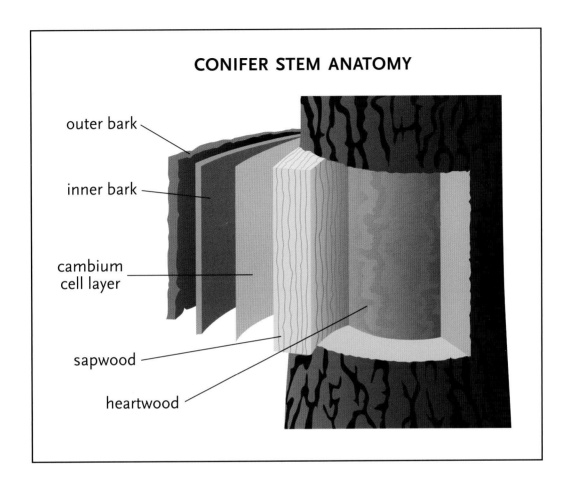

CONIFER STEM ANATOMY

outer bark

inner bark

cambium
cell layer

sapwood

heartwood

together by a chemical called lignin. It is the strongest part of the tree. Surrounding the heartwood is a layer of sapwood, or new cellulose. Sapwood contains xylem, the tissue that carries water upward through the plant.

Sandwiched between the bark on the outside of the plant and the wood on the inside is a layer made up of cambium cells. Although it is the thinnest layer, the cambium cell layer is the source of the plant's growth. Each year it forms a new layer of sapwood, thickening the stem. Over time, as the new sapwood extends outward, the older sapwood toward the center of the tree dies and becomes part of the heartwood. The cambium cell

Climbing the world's big trees is a form of recreation that demands caution—and the right equipment. This climber uses ropes, a harness, and clamps to rappel down a massive sequoia trunk in California.

layer also renews the plant's inner bark. As new tissue is added to the inside of the inner bark layer, older tissue hardens and becomes part of the outer bark.

The wood of conifers is called softwood, in contrast to the wood of deciduous trees, which is called hardwood. Many softwoods are easier to cut, shape, and pulp than hardwood. However, some softwoods, such as cedar and Douglas-fir, are actually harder than many hardwoods, and some hardwoods, such as balsa, are quite soft.

The real difference between hardwoods and softwoods lies in the structure of the wood, not its hardness. In hardwood plants (and all other flowering plants, including grasses and herbs), xylem, the tissue that carries water up through the plant, consists of hollow cells that are joined together to form long, unbroken tubes or vessels. Conifers do not have such vessels. In conifers, water travels through tracheids, long narrow cells that overlap one another. Tracheids, which are connected by membranes through which water can pass, are multipurpose cells. They not only transport water but also form the fibers of the wood itself.

A close-up view of the stem of a young conifer shows tracheids, the long vertical cells that form conifer tissue. The tracheids are narrow and compressed in the heartwood, but in the surrounding xylem layer, where water travels through them, they are much larger.

The majority of conifer species follow one basic growth plan: a single, straight stem with fairly straight branches that stick out to the sides. Some conifers continue to produce new branches near the bottoms of their stems for as long as they live. In many of the larger species, however, branching stops at a certain point in the tree's growth. The stem continues to grow taller, with the result that the mature tree is a tall, bare stem with a high crown of branches and foliage. Nearly all conifers have a growth characteristic that botanists call apical dominance. This means that the apex, or tip of the stem, continues to grow upward throughout the plant's life, and

The cone-shaped, pointed outline of larch trees is typical of many conifer species. These larches are beginning to turn yellow and will soon shed their leaves for winter.

it remains higher than any of the branches. Apical dominance is why many conifers have pointed shapes.

Not all conifers follow the basic growth plan, however. Some species take the form of shrubs, which have two or more stems. A few species have branches that curl or twist. Others, such as *Cedrus atlantica,* the Atlas cedar

Not all conifers raise pointed crowns to the sky. Creeping juniper follows what plant experts call a prostrate growth pattern, which means that it remains low and grows along the ground.

of North Africa, form drooping, tentlike shapes. *Juniperus horizontalis*, the creeping juniper, is one of several species that grow along the ground, forming broad, spreading mats or mounds. Small, slow-growing conifers are called dwarf conifers if they grow from 3 to 6 inches (7.5 to 15.25 cm) a year and miniatures if they grow less than 3 inches (7.5 cm) a year.

Leaves

Dawn redwoods, larches, and bald or swamp cypresses are unusual conifers. They are deciduous, which means that they shed all of their leaves in the fall and remain bare and leafless during the winter. All other conifers are evergreens, plants that have leaves throughout the year. Not all evergreens, however, are conifers. Cycads, eucalypts, and many rainforest trees are evergreens that are not conifers.

Although evergreen conifers have leaves all the time, they do not have the *same* leaves all the time. They shed old leaves and grow new ones—just not all at once as deciduous trees do. In some evergreen species an individual leaf is shed and replaced after a few months. Other conifers hold on

New leaf growth appears at the tips of a Norway spruce's branches in the spring. By the end of their first year, the new leaves will match the older ones in coloration.

to each leaf for much longer—up to five years for the long-lived bristle-cone pines.

Conifer leaves occur in two basic shapes: needles and scales. Needlelike leaves may be rounded or flattened, short or long. Depending upon the species, the leaves grow in pairs from opposite sides of the stem, or in spirals around the stem, or in clusters at the end of the stem. Scalelike leaves occur in different sizes, but typically they are close together and overlap each other. In some conifers, such as cedars and cypresses, scalelike leaves occur in fan-shaped sprays. Some cypresses and pines have two distinctly different kinds of leaves: one when the plants are young and another when they are mature.

The leaves of conifers are well adapted to extremes of heat, cold, and dryness. They are covered with a thick layer of cuticle, the waxy protective coating found on the leaves of all land plants. Most conifer leaves are some

Short, thick, and flattened or long and grasslike, these leaves belong to the needle category of conifer foliage.

shade of green, but a few species have blue-gray, yellow-green, or brownish-green foliage.

Leaves' purpose is to absorb sunlight for photosynthesis and to take part in the nutrient transfer that keeps the plant alive. Like roots and stems, leaves have vascular tissues: xylem and phloem to transport water and nutrients. They also have tiny openings called stomata. Gases—such as the carbon dioxide that plants need for photosynthesis and the oxygen they release as a byproduct—enter and leave the plant through these pores.

CONIFER REPRODUCTION

Cones are the conifers' most distinctive feature. People sometimes call them "pine cones," although that name applies only to cones from members of the genus *Pinus*. Botanists have a technical term for cones—they call them strobili (a single cone is a strobilus). No matter what they are

Living with Fungi

The majority of the world's plants, including conifers, live in beneficial relationships with allies from the fungus kingdom. These relationships are formed when fungi in the soil colonize the root systems of the plants. The result is an association called a mycorrhiza, from the Greek words for "fungus" and "root."

A mycorrhiza consists of threadlike strands of fungus, called hyphae, that have attached themselves to roots. In an ectomycorrhiza (*ecto-* means "outside") the hyphae cover the surfaces of the roots and insert themselves between the root cells, but they do not penetrate the cell walls. In an endomycorrhiza (*endo-* means "inside") the hyphae enter the walls of the cells, where they form bubbles, swellings, or branching tubes. These structures increase the area of contact between the hyphae and the interiors of the cell walls.

A mycorrhiza is a symbiosis, a relationship that benefits both partners. Mycorrhizal symbiosis works because materials such as nutrients can pass between the hyphae and the plant cells. The fungus benefits by receiving food in the form of sugars that the plant has produced through photosynthesis. In addition, the plant's roots give the fungus a substrate, or surface on which to grow. The plant benefits because the fungus spreads through the surrounding soil and functions like an enlargement of the root. Through this enlarged surface area the mycorrhiza can absorb more water and mineral nutrients than the plant could absorb through its roots alone. By increasing plants'ability to absorb necessary nutrients such as nitrogen, phosphorus, and potassium, mycorrhizae help conifers and other plants survive in soils that are poor in nutrients.

In some cases the fungus partner in a mycorrhiza may do more than simply absorb nutrients from the soil—it may attract them. Researchers at the University of Guelph in Ontario, Canada, found that up to a quarter of the nitrogen in some Eastern white pines came from soil-dwelling insects and springtails (tiny insectlike creatures) that had been lured to the roots by chemicals in the tre e s' mycorrhizal fungi, then killed by toxins given off by the fungi. As the creatures decayed, the mycorrhizae absorbed nitrogen from their bodies, and the nitrogen made its way into the plants.

Fossils show that mycorrhizae existed 400 million years ago, early in the history of land plants. Over the ages conifers and other plants have evolved not just alongside fungi, but in close association with them.

The outer layer of this small pine tree root, seen under a microscope in cross-section, is a coat of fungus. The fungus has covered the surface of the root, forming a common and beneficial partnership called a mycorrhiza.

Most conifers bear their seeds in woody cones, such as the mature cone of a Norway spruce (left) and the smaller developing cones of a cryptomeria or sugi (right). When mature, the sugi's cones will be tough, spiky, and round.

called, cones are the conifers' method of sexual reproduction, in which two types of reproductive cells join to form the beginning of a new plant.

The cells involved in conifer reproduction are pollen and ovules. The goal of reproduction is to get a grain of pollen to land on an ovule and fertilize the gamete, or sex cell, inside it. A fertilized gamete, or zygote, develops into an embryo contained within a seed. If that seed lands on the ground under the right conditions, it will germinate, which means that it will start to grow. To accomplish this mission, conifers rely on cones, wind, and, in a few cases, birds and animals.

Both pollen and ovules develop on organs called cones. The two kinds of cones, however, are very different. Pollen cones are small and inconspicuous. They can be difficult to see unless you look for them carefully in the spring. Once the pollen cones have released their fine, dustlike pollen to be carried away by the wind, they shrivel up and disappear.

Wind is vital to the reproduction of many conifers. A breeze blows grains from the pollen cone of a lodgepole pine. If some of the grains land on seed cones, fertilized ovules, or seeds, may result.

Ovulate cones, or seed cones, also start out small, soft, and inconspicuous. They consist of one or more scales bearing ovules. Some species have several hundred scales and many ovules; others have just a few ovules, or one, per cone. When the cones are new, the scales are parted to expose the ovules to passing pollen. Once the season of pollination is over, however, the scales grow together around the fertilized ovules. The seed cone closes, and then it grows as the seeds ripen, becoming the large, woody cone that people associate with conifers.

It can take as little as a couple of months or as long as three or four years for conifer seeds to ripen. When the seeds are ripe and ready to be released into the world, the cone breaks apart or opens so that the seeds

The small, berrylike seed cones of yews are partly enclosed in a soft coating called an aril. Thrushes, waxwings, and other birds eat the arils, then spread the seed in their droppings.

can fall out. Some seeds have structures called wings, small sheets of woody or papery material that let them glide on the breeze. For these conifer species, wind is the primary dispersal mechanism—the thing that carries seeds away from parent plants. Yews, plum-yews, and junipers use a different dispersal mechanism. Their seeds are partially enclosed in pulpy coverings that attract birds and animals. The creatures eat the berry-like cones and later spread the plants' seeds in their droppings.

Nearly all conifer species are monoecious, a botanical term that means that each plant produces both kinds of sex cells. In the case of conifers, this

Like most conifers, the pitch pine bears pollen and seed cones on the same tree. A pollen cone (sometimes called a male cone) is on the left, an immature seed (or female) cone on the right. The cones have formed among new leaves at the ends of branches, with older, longer leaves behind them.

means that pollen cones and seed cones develop on the same trees. The conifers can fertilize their own ovules (self-pollinate), and they can also fertilize and be fertilized by other plants (cross-pollination). From the point of view of a species, cross-pollination is desirable because it lets favorable traits, such as resistance to insects, spread among a population. To increase the chances of cross-pollination, some monoecious conifers produce their pollen cones and seed cones on different parts of the tree, or at slightly different seasons.

A few conifer species are dioecious, which means that each plant produces only pollen cones or only seed cones. To reproduce, these plants must be near others of their species so that pollen can make the journey between trees.

ECOLOGY

Ecology refers to the network of relationships and interactions among organisms and their shared environment. Conifers interact with their environment in many ways, some of which scientists are just beginning to understand.

Conifers provide nesting sites for many birds and for small animals such as squirrels. The plants are food sources, too, either directly for birds that eat conifer seeds or indirectly for birds that eat insects they find in the conifers' bark. Scientists have discovered that connections between birds and conifers can be complex. Pinyon jays, Clark's nutcrackers, and Mexican jays, for example, are birds that eat the seeds of pinyon pines, which grow in Mexico and the American Southwest. (Pinyon seeds, sometimes called pine nuts, are one of the few kinds of conifer seed that humans also use as food.) The birds gather stockpiles of seeds and store them in holes in the ground. The birds do not always eat all of the seeds they collect, which means that some of the seeds have a chance to germinate, resulting in more trees to produce more seeds.

The grubs of bark beetles have gnawed out this gallery of tunnels beneath the bark of a Douglas-fir.

Conifers are also the favored foods of many destructive insect pests. The spruce budworm, for example, is the larva of a small moth. It devours the leaves, twigs, and young cones of spruce trees, as well as other conifers. The spruce budworm has killed large tracts of spruce and fir forest in North America.

Other notable conifer pests are bark beetles. The grubs, or immature forms, of these insects gnaw their way through the soft inner bark of lodge-pole pines, Western hemlocks, spruces, and many other conifers, leaving behind the branching networks of trails known as galleries. If such damage is severe, the tree dies. Trees can defend themselves from a small-scale attack by producing resin that drowns the beetles and fills their holes. When a lot of beetles attack a tree at once, however, the tree cannot respond quickly enough. The insects bore into the tree in many places and lay their eggs inside. When the eggs hatch, the grubs begin feeding.

Parasites such as fungi and bacteria infect conifers and cause many kinds of plant diseases, including cankers, blights, rots, galls, stains, and rusts. Plants called dwarf mistletoes also parasitize conifers. These ball-shaped or tufted plants attach themselves to the bark of a tree and then send long, rootlike strings of tissue through the bark and into the sapwood, draining off the tree's nutrients and water and introducing destructive bacteria from the outside world. Dwarf mistletoe has been especially damaging to conifer forests in the American West, where some forest managers regard it as a more serious problem than fungal infections or beetle attacks.

A less harmful kind of ecological interaction exists between conifers and the many varieties of fungus that live in the plants' root systems. These are the fungi that form mycorrhizae, unions of fungi and plant roots that benefit both sides. The close link between certain species of conifers and fungi means that mushrooms, the reproductive organs of fungi, are often found growing near those trees. The Douglas-fir forests of the Pacific Northwest, for example, are a good place to find chanterelles, edible mushrooms that grow in association with these conifers.

Conifers also interact with the elements. Stands of closely growing conifers form windbreaks that protect other, more fragile vegetation from wind damage. Yet strong winds can topple even massive conifers, creating openings in the forest where smaller plants can receive sunlight. Many conifers thrive in cold regions, and they are adapted to harsh conditions. Snow slides off their conelike shapes, and their branches are are somewhat flexible, able to bend under the weight of snow or ice. Severe loads of snow and ice, though, can snap branches and even stems.

Fire plays a part in the lives of conifers. Each year, forest fires sweep through the forests of western North America and other regions where dry, resinous conifers burst readily into flame. Yet although such fires are terrifying and destructive, they are also part of the natural life cycle of the forests. Forest managers have learned, in fact, that when they put out every fire as quickly as possible, the result is a dangerous build-up of flammable material.

Four years after a fire in Yellowstone National Park, young lodgepole pines spring up beside charred trunks. Thin-barked lodgepole pines are easily killed by fire, which removes old trees and any diseases or parasites they carry. New trees appear quickly in the open, sunny, burned-over areas.

Some fires sweep swiftly across the forest floor, or through the crowns of the trees, leaving many trees singed but alive. Mature red pines and Ponderosa pines, for example, have thick, corklike, fire-resistant bark that protects them from minor fires.

Ponderosa pines, which form dry open, parklike forests across parts of the West, do not just tolerate fire. They benefit from it. Without frequent surface fires to remove fallen trees and small young pines that compete with established trees for space and nutrients, mature Ponderosa pines cannot reach their full growth. The Monterey pine also needs fire. It is what scientists call a serotinous plant, one that releases its seeds only after a fire. This ensures that the newly released seeds will fall on ground that has been cleared, where they will be able to take root and grow without much competition. Many pines are serotinous, and so is the giant sequoia.

As scientists learn more about the fire ecology of Ponderosa pines and other conifers around the world, forest managers are modifying some of their practices. New forestry principles call for allowing some fires to burn. Forest management, however, is a delicate balance between preserving valuable trees (as well as other property such as homes and businesses) and letting nature run its course.

THE TAIGA

Conifers are found on every continent except Antarctica and on many islands. Nowhere in the world, though, do they dominate the environment as much as in the forests of the far north. These northern forests are a biome—a major community of living things that have adapted to a particular environment.

Scientists usually classify biomes according to the dominant type of vegetation, such as wetlands, grasslands, or forests. The world's largest terrestrial biome, covering about 17 percent of the plant's land masses, is the belt of northern forest that stretches across Siberia, Alaska, Canada, and northern Europe. This biome is sometimes called the boreal forest (boreal means "northern," from Boreas, the ancient Greek god of the north wind). Another name for this biome is taiga, from the Russian word for "forest."

The taiga has long cold winters and short wet summers. It is an environment of extremes, where temperatures can reach -65 degrees Fahrenheit (-54 degrees Celsius) in the winter. In some parts of the taiga there just fifty days a year when the temperature does not fall below the freezing point. Some deciduous trees, including birch, alder, willow, and aspen, manage to grow in this inhospitable environment, although specimens that grow in the taiga are much smaller than those farther south. Far more numerous, however, are the conifers. They blanket the taiga in vast numbers.

The boreal forest or taiga stretches across the cool northern reaches of Eurasia and North America. Made up mostly of conifers, this belt of forest is the largest biome in the world.

Moose browse a taiga meadow in Canada's Yukon Territory. The demand for wood products is driving logging operations into the boreal forest, raising questions about the fate of the taiga and its inhabitants.

Balsam fir, black spruce, Siberian spruce, jack pine, white spruce, and white fir are among the conifers that make up the boreal forest. They provide habitat for a wide array of wildlife: wolves, wolverines, weasels, bears, foxes, lynxes, small rodents such as voles and lemmings, eagles, ravens, owls, and many other species of birds, some of which migrate to the taiga each summer to breed.

For years, the taiga was safe from much human interference because it is such a cold and difficult environment and because it has few highways or industrial centers. Today, however, as forests disappear from more temperate parts of the world, the taiga has become a tempting source of wood to meet the world's demands for newspaper, toilet paper, cardboard, plywood, construction materials, and other softwood products.

Although the taiga is one of only a few large stretches of ancient forest left on earth, little of it is protected by conservation measures such as national parks. Clearcutting, in which loggers cut down every tree in a large tract, is already taking place in many parts of the taiga, and conservation experts warn that the fate of this northern forest will soon be decided. Like other plants, animals, and environments from whales to rainforests, the conifers of the taiga are caught in a tug of war between economic demands and the urge to preserve.

Native Americans of the northern Pacific coast carved conifer trunks into images with spiritual and symbolic meaning. Known as totem poles, the carvings—such as this one made by the Tlingit people—are one of many uses that these Native Americans found for the trees among which they lived.

People and Conifers

Before the Spanish conquered Mexico in the sixteenth century, the Native Americans of central Mexico regarded *Pinus teocote,* a pine tree, as the tree of the gods. They burned its resin in sacred rituals. Across the Pacific Ocean the Buriats, a Mongolian people living in Siberia, believed that groves of *Pinus sylvestris* were sacred places. When they rode through the groves they stayed silent, so that their voices would not offend the gods.

In 1775, on the eve of American independence, the colonists decorated several of their flags with images of Eastern white pine trees, symbols of the forests that supported the growing American shipbuilding industry. The flag of modern Lebanon features *Cedrus libani,* the Lebanon cedar, a tree that has been famous since biblical times, when its fragrant red wood was used in the building of palaces and temples. The people of southern Brazil have adopted the silhouette of an Araucaria called the Parana pine as a regional symbol, incorporating it in everything from sidewalk designs to paintings.

Europeans have incorporated conifers into their art since the days of the ancient Greeks and Romans. Pine cones were a common theme in the walls paintings of Roman houses, and in the first century C.E. a Roman

Vincent Van Gogh painted *Road with Cypress and Star* in 1890. Some art critics think that the tall cypress tree represents a bridge between the earth and the heavens.

bronze worker made a fountain in the shape of a huge pine cone; it stands today in a courtyard of the Vatican Museum. More recently, Dutch painter Vincent Van Gogh wrote to his brother Theodore in 1899, "I am totally preoccupied with the cypress. . . . I find it strange that they have never been painted in the way that I see them." Cypress trees appear in some of Van Gogh's most admired paintings.

People in many times and places have celebrated conifers, perhaps because they are evergreens. Because these trees never lose their leaves, they have become symbols of eternal life. Or perhaps the affection for conifers stems from the fact that they are very useful plants.

THE USES OF CONIFERS

The value of certain kinds of conifer wood was recognized thousands of years ago, when timber made from the cedars of Lebanon—prized for its fragrance and its rich red color—was used in the building of palaces and temples in the Middle East. Throughout the centuries people have used conifer wood as fuel and also as material for building houses, ships, bridges, and furniture. Wood is still used for construction and, in some places, for fuel. Today, however, much of the softwood harvested around the world is pulped, or turned into a soft cellulose mash that can be made into paper or cardboard.

Conifers yield many products other than wood. Live plants, grown on tree farms or in nurseries, are sold for use in landscaping and ornamental gardening. People have carried species of conifers around the world for use in gardens. The monkey puzzle tree, for example, traveled from South America to North America and Europe because plant collectors and nursery growers thought that it would make an interesting, exotic garden tree.

Bonsai, a special form of gardening that originated in China, makes use of conifers as well as flowering trees. Bonsai gardeners employ techniques of trimming, wiring, and root control to produce tiny versions of

Conifers such as this white pine are often used in bonsai, an Asian art of gardening with miniature forms of trees. Artworks and ancient texts from China and Japan suggest that people have practiced bonsai for more than a thousand years.

full-sized trees. Junipers, pines, yews, and cryptomeria are among the conifers that lend themselves to bonsai gardening.

Conifers have served as food sources. Pine nuts and some other seeds are edible, as are the cambium and inner bark of certain species. Native Americans in the Canadian province of British Columbia traditionally ate the inner bark of Western hemlock and lodgepole pine. They scraped it off the inside of the bark, cooked it, pounded it, and shaped it into cakes that could be stored for a long time. Soaking the cakes in water produced a nourishing food. Bark was a food source for other North American native peoples as well, including the Adirondacks of New York State. Native peoples around the world have also made dyes and traditional medicines from the bark of various conifer species.

Resin has long been an economically important product of conifers. People have harvested it for thousands of years, using unprocessed resin in traditional medicines, paints, varnishes, and also as an ingredient in certain alcoholic beverages, such as the Greek drink retsina. Most modern commercial uses of resin, however, use distilled pine resin. The distilling process turns resin into two substances, the liquid turpentine and a hard, glassy substance called rosin. Turpentine is an ingredient in a multitude of products,

Les Landes is a region of France that was planted in the nineteenth century with pine forests for industrial use. There foresters harvest resin by tapping the trunks of *Pinus pinaster,* the maritime pine.

including varnishes, dyes, inks, and adhesives. Rosin is used in the manufacture of paper, soap, rubber and other goods.

The resin of kauri trees, members of the araucaria family, is known as copal. Used as an ingredient in some inks, paints, and varnishes, copal is a source of cash for people in the Philippines and Papua New Guinea who harvest it from the forests.

ECONOMICS AND THE ENVIRONMENT

The economic usefulness of conifers sometimes clashes with environmental concerns. One example of this conflict has been playing out in the Pacific Northwest, where the ecological tie between conifer trees and a small owl has made headlines for years.

The northern spotted owl lives in the Canadian province of British Columbia and in the states of Washington, Oregon, and California. Its habitat is old-growth forest, where mature conifers such as redwoods, Douglas-firs, and spruces offer room for the owls to fly under the canopy of leaves, as well as cavities that the owls can use for nesting. Unfortunately for the owls, that type of habitat is exactly the kind of forest that attracts logging companies. The large trees of old-growth forest yield more timber and pulp than younger, smaller trees.

The northern spotted owl is listed as "threatened" under the U.S. Endangered Species Act. As a result, the U.S. Fish and Wildlife Service (USFWS) is required to work with local governments, representatives of industry, biologists, and conservation groups to develop a plan for protecting enough habitat to allow the species to recover, or increase its numbers. Logging interests and conservationists, however, have been unable to agree on what is "enough" habitat to save the bird—or, in some cases, whether the bird should be saved. At the same time, scientists have discovered that the spotted owl now faces a second threat from eastern

Logs lie stacked and ready for transport at the edge of a clearcut in a conifer forest. Ever-growing demand for paper, timber, and other wood products puts pressure on such forests worldwide.

Northern spotted owls perch in an old-growth forest in Oregon. These birds are at the center of a long-raging conflict over forest use.

barred owls, which are moving west into new territory and competing with the spotted owls for habitat.

The northern spotted owl was added to the Endangered Species list in 1990. In 2007 the USFWS released its most recent version of the recovery plan for scientists to review. At that time researchers for the conservation group Defenders of Wildlife estimated that fewer than 2,500 pairs of northern spotted owls remained.

The plight of the northern spotted owl is not a simple story of a threatened bird pitted against greedy loggers. Timber companies represent not just corporate profits but also jobs that support loggers, sawmill workers, and their families. They provide products, such as paper and wood, that the general public consumes in great quantities.

Conservationists, however, are right to point out that saving the spotted owl is only part of the reason that logging in old-growth conifer forests should be carefully considered and controlled. Such forests cannot be replaced by farms. They are complex ecosystems that house hundreds of different kinds of organisms and have developed over hundreds of years. Like other cases around the world, the conflict over the northern spotted owl highlights the importance of conifers in two worlds: natural and human.

There are only 600 or so species of conifers, but these trees form vast forests. Their importance to the natural world, and to human life, is too big to measure.

Evergreens on the Red List

The World Conservation Union (IUCN) is an international association of conservation organizations. Each year it publishes a Red List of endangered and threatened plants and animals around the world. The 2007 Red List showed 21 conifer species in the IUCN's most serious category: critically endangered. Another 53 species were classed as endangered, while 96 were labeled vulnerable, or at risk of becoming endangered. Together the three categories had 170 species, more than a quarter of all conifers.

Six members of the pine family are critically endangered, as are four podocarp species. Four members of the cypress family are also considered critically endangered. One of them is the dawn redwood; the coast redwood and the giant sequoia are both classed as vulnerable.

What does the future hold for endangered conifers? Universities, botanical gardens, and conservation organizations are cooperating to create plant "arks" like the Millennium Seed Bank at Britain's Royal Botanical Gardens. Such sites can preserve trees, seeds, and DNA samples from endangered species in protected conditions, in case the species are driven to extinction in the wild. Other conservation activities are aimed at habitat protection for conifers and at sustainable harvests of conifers and their products, with the goal of preserving these ancient plants in their wild glory.

adapt—To change or develop in ways that aid survival in the environment.

anatomy—The physical structure of an organism.

angiosperm—Flowering plant in which the seed develops inside a protective structure called a carpel, which is the female reproductive organ of the flower.

aquatic—Having to do with water; living in water (fresh or salt).

botany—The scientific study of plants.

conservation—Action or movement aimed at protecting and preserving wildlife or its habitat.

ethnobotany—The study of how various cultures and societies have used plants.

evolution—The pattern of change in life-forms over time, as new species, or types of plants and animals, develop from old ones.

evolve—To change over time.

extinct—No longer existing; died out.

genetic—Having to do with genes, material made of DNA inside the cells of living organisms. Genes carry information about inherited characteristics from parents to offspring and determine the form of each organism.

germinate—To begin to grow.

gymnosperm—A seed plant that produces seeds that do not develop inside a protective carpel, as the seeds of angiosperms or flowering plants do; cycads, ginkgos, and conifers are gymnosperms.

organism—Any living thing.

paleobotany—The study of ancient plants, mainly through fossils.

paleontology—The study of ancient life, mainly through fossils.

parasite—Organism that feeds on, and often lives on or inside, another organism; the relationship benefits the parasite but is neutral or harmful to the host.

phloem—Specialized tissue that carries glucose made through photosynthesis from the plant's leaves to other parts of its structure.

photosynthesis—The process by which plants with specialized structures called chloroplasts in the cells of their leaves make food (in the form of the sugar glucose) from water, sunlight, and carbon dioxide.

plant—A multicelled organism made up of complex cells (with a nucleus and other internal structures inside each cell) that makes its own food through photosynthesis.

resin—A thick, sticky liquid produced by some plants, including many conifers.

shrub—A low-growing, woody plant with multiple stems.

symbiosis—A relationship in which two organisms live in close contact, each providing some benefit to the other.

taxonomy—The scientific system for classifying living things, grouping them in categories according to similarities and differences, and naming them.

terrestrial—Living on the land.

vascular—Having specialized tissues that allow water and other nutrients to move through the plant's structure.

woody—Having wood or barklike tissue on stems and branches.

xylem—Specialized tissue that carries water upward from a plant's roots to its leaves.

CONIFER

DIVISION

CLASS

ORDER

FAMILY   Podocarpaceae   Araucariaceae   Cupressaceae
                (podocarps or   (araucarias)   (cypresses)
                yellow-woods)

SUBFAMILY

FAMILY TREE

CONIFEROPHYTA

Pinopsida
(4 orders − 3 extinct)

Pinales (living conifers)

Sciadopityaceae
(umbrella pine)

Taxaceae
(yews)

Cephalotaxaceae
(plum-yews)

Pinaceae
(pines and others)

Abietoideae
(firs, cedars, hemlocks)

Laricoideae
(larches, Douglas-firs)

Piceoideae
(spruces)

Pinoideae
(pines)

FIND OUT MORE

FURTHER READING

Preston, Richard. *Wild Trees: A Story of Passion and Daring.* New York: Random House, 2007.

Robinson, Richard, editor. *Plant Sciences.* New York: Macmillan Reference, 2001.

Stefoff, Rebecca. *The Flowering Plant Division.* Tarrytown, NY: Marshall Cavendish Benchmark, 2006.

WEB SITES

http://conifersociety.org
The Web site of the American Conifer Society has a photo gallery, a database of conifer varieties, and links to sites featuring conifer gardens.

http://www.conifers.org/zz/pinales.htm
The Pinophyta page of the excellent, illustrated online Gymnosperm Database offers information on the taxonomy, life cycles, and economic and social uses of conifers; the site includes detailed pages about each of the seven families of conifers, as well as ginkgos, cycads, and gnetophytes.

http://www.usna.usda.gov/Gardens/collections/conifer.html
The U.S. National Arboretum's Web site features a virtual tour of the USNA's seven-acre collection of dwarf and slow-growing conifers.

http://www.fao.org/docrep/X0453E/X0453e00.htm
The Forestry Department of the United Nations Food and Agriculture Organization (FAO) produced this report on the distribution of conifers and their economic uses (other than as wood); it describes the uses of conifers in food, art, and gardening.

http://www.pbs.org/wgbh/nova/methuselah
This companion site to the PBS program "Methuselah Tree" provides a virtual view of the world's oldest living thing, a bristlecone pine known as Methuselah.

http://www.botany.org/resources/botany.php
The Botanical Society of America's "What Is Botany?" page offers an overview of the scientific study of plants, including conifers; it also has information about botanical careers in areas ranging from ethnobotany to forest resource management.

http://www.blueplanetbiomes.org/taiga.htm
Taiga Biomes is a concise overview of the plants, animals, and climate of the taiga, the northern coniferous forest that is the largest land biome on the planet.

The author found these sources especially helpful when researching this book.

Beerling, David. *The Emerald Planet: How Plants Changed Earth's History.* New York: Oxford University Press, 2007.

Ingrouille, Martin J., and Bill Eddie. *Plants: Evolution and Diversity.* Cambridge, UK: Cambridge University Press, 2006.

Lamb, Frank H. *Sagas of the Evergreens: The Story and the Economic, Social, and Cultural Contribution of the Evergreen Trees and Forests of the World.* New York: Norton, 1938.

Mikolajski, Andrew. *Conifers.* New York: Lorenz Books, 1997.

Niklas, Karl J. *The Evolutionary Biology of Plants.* Chicago: University of Chicago Press, 1997.

Pielou, E.C. *The World of Northern Evergreens.* Ithaca: Comstock Publishing/Cornell University Press, 1988.

Van Gelderen, D.M. *Conifers: The Illustrated Encyclopedia.* 2 volumes. Portland, OR: Timber Press, 1996.

Willis, K.J., and J.C. McElwain. *The Evolution of Plants.* New York: Oxford University Press, 2002.

I N D E X

Page numbers in **boldface** are illustrations.

ABOUT THE AUTHOR

Rebecca Stefoff is the author of many books on scientific subjects for young readers. She has explored the world of plants and animals in Marshall Cavendish's Living Things and AnimalWays series, and she has authored several books in the Family Trees series, including *The Flowering Plant Division*. Stefoff has also written about evolution in *Charles Darwin and the Evolution Revolution* (Oxford University Press, 1996), and she appeared in the *A&E Biography* program on Darwin and his work. Stefoff lives in Portland, Oregon. You can learn more about her books for young readers at www.rebeccastefoff.com.